Pogo
The Puppy Mill Dog
(A Rescue Tale)
This book is based on the true story of Pogo who we adopted
from a rescue center called Carolina Poodle Rescue (CPR)
(www.CarolinaPoodleRescue.org)
All profits from this book are used to support the amazing
on-going work of this non-profit organization and their staff (like
Jessie Morgan who is mentioned in the story). Their mission is:
"One By One, Until There Are None."

We Want to give special recognition to:
.The caring volunteers (Jennifer Smith and Phyllis Rathbone) who
refused to accept Pogo's initial diagnosis of a significantly
shortened life and pushed to find a solution that would
increase her life by 8-10 years
.The Cardiology Department veterinarian ("Dr. D") and her staff at
North Carolina State Veterinary School who diagnosed and
repaired Pogo's heart and donated ALL funding for her very
complex surgery.

Our sincere hope is that you will consider adopting from a
rescue center.

Written By: Fred & Jeri Abrams
Illustrated By: Sarah Sellers
Graphic Design by Jared Sellers
Copyright: 2017 All Rights Reserved
ISBN: 978-0692933428

Hi! I am Pogo the Cock-a-Poo, and for as long as I can remember my home was a small wire cage. The wire floor hurt my feet. There was barely enough room to turn around.

I live at what people call a "puppy mill" with a lot of other dogs living in identical cages. All of us sleep on the wire floor of our cages.

A man comes around once a day and gives me food and water. I almost never get to leave my cage. I long for someone to touch or pet me.

The worst part of my life is when the man comes and takes all my puppies away from me. I never get to see them again and I am very sad. It only gets better when I have some more puppies. I always feel tired and weak. My fur is all matted and dirty.

One day the man didn't come with the food and water. I was worried. Then a woman came around to the cages, took all of us out and put us together in other tiny cages. She sounded very angry. She loaded all of the cages in a truck and I heard her telling someone the man had died and she needed to get rid of all the dogs.

She drove us to a place with a lot of other dogs
and dropped us off telling them to get rid of us -
we were all very scared. There was a smell of death
in this new place. I felt very tired.

After a couple of days I heard a very sweet lady's voice in the next room asking about "the puppy mill dogs." They opened the cage of six of us to take us to the other room. I ran out of the cage.

I ran as fast as I could toward the other room - I had never been able to run living in the tiny cage. As I went through the door I tried to turn toward the lady and slid sideways across the floor. The nice lady named Jesse laughed.

I ran to her. She picked me up, held me close, and petted me. That was the happiest I had ever been in my life. She offered me a very yummy little piece of food - she called it a treat. She had one hand on my chest and said to someone that my heart felt like a diesel engine - whatever that is.

Jessie put me and the other dogs in our own little cages with a soft blanket on the bottom. She loaded us into her car. I was so tired from all the excitement that I fell asleep. I was more comfortable than I had ever been in my life.

Jessie took all of us to a place called the "poodle farm" and gave us a nice place to sleep and play. They gave me a bath and cut my tangled fur. There was plenty of food and water. People talked softly to us and petted us.

The play area felt very strange on my feet. The people called it grass - I was very scared to walk on this grass after living in the cage. I had always gone potty in my cage and these people wanted me to go on the grass. They were so nice I wanted to make them happy.

A nice lady named Jennifer took me to someone they called "the vet". He looked in my mouth and ears, and put something up to my chest to listen to my heart. The vet told Jennifer that I had a hole in my heart. They said it was very serious, and that I was a very sick little dog who might not live much longer. They said I needed a special doctor to make me better.

Miss Jennifer took me to a special doctor named Dr. D who talked softly to me and petted me. She said she could fix my heart hole and wanted to start right away! The next thing I remember, I was waking up with a cone on my neck. I wanted to bite and lick my leg, but couldn't reach it. Miss Jennifer came back and held me. Dr D told her the hole was closed and that I would start feeling a lot better soon!

They left me alone while they talked and I got the
cone off my head. I chewed on my leg where it felt
funny. I found something hard and ate it. The vet
did something called x-rays and talked about
the hard staples I had swallowed.

I went to Miss Jennifer's home to rest; for some reason she was really interested in my poop for the next few days. She seemed very happy when I yelped while pooping and she found the staples.

I have worried that maybe my puppies might have the same heart problems too. I hope they are all happy and healthy. I still worry about them.

After awhile Miss Jennifer took the cone off and I was able to lick my leg. Another nice lady named Phyllis came to see me and asked if I would like to come stay at her house for awhile. They called her a foster mom and she told me she had dogs and a cat. I tried to make friends with the cat but he seemed afraid of me.

One day a man and woman came to visit me. They had a red cock-a-poo named Rusty. I spent several nights with Rusty and the new people. They spoke softly to me and petted me a lot. I gave them lots of kisses and rolled over to let them rub my tummy. That felt really good.

I decided to choose them as my "furever" family because Rusty told me he needed a sister. They put both of us in their car and we drove a long time. They held me and petted me a lot.

When we got to Rusty's home they let me run around the house and lay down on things called a couch and bed which was really soft. The first night I got to sleep with them in the bed and snuggle up to them. I liked to give them kisses and they gave me lots of tummy rubs.

It was very scary when they put on my leash
and took me to the back yard to potty on
the grass. I ran in circles around them and
jumped at every sound.

I love to jump around and run from one room to another. My humans call these my "ninja moves" when I jump from one place to another. I still slide sideways when I try to run fast around corners in the house.

I like to hide in the pillows on their bed.
Especially when they want me to go outside.

Rusty is nice to me most of the time. Except when he finds something he wants for his very own - then he's pretty grumpy with everyone if he thinks they are going to take it away. I just ignore him when he's like that. Other times we play together. He taught me how to beg for table scraps.

I am so thankful to have my "furever" home and humans who like to pet me and rub my tummy. I reward them with lots of kisses. I especially like to sleep snuggled up to my dad's head and wake him with kisses on top of his head where he doesn't have any fur.

I feel so sorry for all the dogs who still live in cages at puppy mills. I am so thankful for people like those at the "poodle farm" and the doctors who gave me a healed heart! I hope you can find a special dog like me to rescue like my humans did.

The wonderful shelter where we got Pogo is
Carolina Poodle Rescue (CPR) (www.carolinapoodlerescue.org)

We cannot say enough good about CPR and all the other rescue
shelters that work so hard to find animals their "furever" homes.
Following CPR on their FaceBook page continually renews our faith
in humanity as they find transport for rescued dogs, attend to
medical issues, provide lifetime care for senior dogs, and arrange
adoptions.

This is book two in "a rescue tale" series.

66975601R00034

Made in the USA
Lexington, KY
29 August 2017